Raffi
Baby Beluga Book

When I first met a beluga whale
at the Vancouver Aquarium,
it was love at first sight!

McClelland and Stewart

McClelland and Stewart Limited
The Canadian Publishers
25 Hollinger Road
Toronto, Ontario
M4B 3G2

Canadian Cataloguing in Publication Data
Raffi.
    Baby beluga book
ISBN 0-07710-7261-9 (bound). ISBN 0-7710-7260-0 (pbk).
1. Children's songs. I. Title.
M1990.R33   784.6'2406   C83-094039-1

Credits
SONGS
BABY BELUGA
Words and music by Raffi and Debi Pike
© 1980 Homeland Publishing (CAPAC)

BISCUITS IN THE OVEN
Words and music by Bill Russell
© 1980 Homeward Publishing (PROC) and
Egos Anonymous (PROC)

OATS AND BEANS AND BARLEY GROW
Traditional

DAY-O
Traditional

THANKS A LOT
Words and music by Raffi
© Homeland Publishing (CAPAC)

TO EVERYONE IN ALL THE WORLD
Traditional, French translation by Lise Poitras

ALL I REALLY NEED
Music by Raffi, Debi Pike, Bonnie and Bert Simpson
© 1980 Homeland Publishing (CAPAC)

OVER IN THE MEADOW
Music traditional, lyrics by Lee Hays and Doris Kaplan
© 1968 by Sanga Music Inc.
All rights reserved. Used by permission.

THIS OLD MAN
Traditional, adapted by Raffi, Debi Pike, Bonnie
and Bert Simpson
© 1980 Homeland Publishing (CAPAC)

KUMBAYA
Traditional

JOSHUA GIRAFFE
Words and music by Pat Godfrey and Dennis Pendrith,
adapted by Raffi
© 1980 Homeward Publishing (PROC) and
Apparition Music (PROC)

MORNINGTOWN RIDE
Words and music by Malvina Reynolds
© 1959 Amadeo Music
International copyright secured. Used by permission.

ILLUSTRATIONS
Jane Fernandes – 9, 10, 11, 26, 27. Franklin Hammond – cover, 7, 8, 36, 37, 38, 39, 40, 41, 42, 43, 45, 47, 48.
Vladyana Krykorka – 12, 13, 14, 28, 30, 31. Maryann Kovalski – 32, 33, 34. Barb Reid – 16, 17, 20.
James Tughan – title page, 22.

PHOTOGRAPHY
John Harquail – cover, 46, 47, 48. Vancouver Sun – reference title page.

DESIGN
Franklin Hammond.

Printed and bound in Canada

To Kavna

Contents

Note to Parents and Teachers

Early experiences with oral and written language contribute to children's readiness for and progress in developing reading skills. Young children quickly and naturally become familiar with the words of Raffi's songs by listening to and singing along with his records.

Very small children will enjoy turning these pages, delighting in the pictures and producing the lyrics from memory. Five- and six-year-olds, who have begun to learn to read, will find it easy and fun to recognize the words to a favourite song in print.

All the words to all the songs from *Baby Beluga* have been reproduced here in large type. Coloured borders around the lyrics (blue for side 1 of the record, orange for side 2) make them easy to locate. Choruses also have been printed in a bright colour so that children can quickly refer back to them whenever they see the word CHORUS.

Chords are shown above the melody so that the songs may be accompanied on guitar, autoharp, or ukulele.

Acknowledgements

My co-authors, Bert Simpson, Bonnie Simpson, and Debi Pike, played a major part in the conception and writing of the book. They originated the idea of developing the book as an early reader. On nearly every aspect of this work I sought their advice. *Baby Beluga Book* is very much *our* book.

Thanks to Toivo Kiil for believing in this project and supporting it from the outset. Thanks also to Franklin Hammond for his sensitive art direction. He cared for this book in a special way. And thanks finally to Judith Owen for her encouragement, patience and valuable contributions. She was a pleasure to work with.

Baby Beluga

Ba - by be - lu - ga in the deep blue sea, swim so wild and you swim so free. Heav - en a - bove and the sea be - low, and a lit - tle white whale on the go. Ba - by be - lu - ga, ba - by be - lu - ga, is the wa - ter warm, is your ma - ma home with you so hap - py?

The beluga Raffi met is named Kavna. She is now twelve years old. Baby belugas are grey when they are born but become almost pure white as they get older. These whales have been called "sea canaries" because of the sounds they make. They whistle, sing, and chatter to each other as they dip and dive under water.

Baby beluga in the deep blue sea,
Swim so wild and you swim so free.
Heaven above and the sea below,
And a little white whale on the go.

> Baby beluga, baby beluga,
> Is the water warm, is your mama home
> With you so happy?

Way down yonder where the dolphins play,
Where you dive and splash all day,
Waves roll in and the waves roll out,
See the water squirtin' out of your spout.

> Baby beluga, oh, baby beluga,
> Sing your little song, sing for all your friends,
> We like to hear you.

When it's dark, you're home and fed,
Curl up snug in your water bed.
Moon is shining and the stars are out,
Good night, little whale, good night.

> Baby beluga, oh, baby beluga,
> With tomorrow's sun, another day's begun,
> You'll soon be waking.

Baby beluga in the deep blue sea,
Swim so wild and you swim so free,
Heaven above and the sea below
And a little white whale on the go—
You're just a little white whale on the go.

Biscuits in the Oven

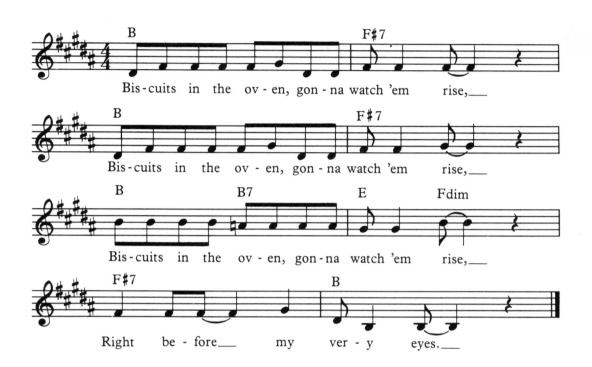

Bis-cuits in the ov-en, gon-na watch 'em rise,___

Bis-cuits in the ov-en, gon-na watch 'em rise,___

Bis-cuits in the ov-en, gon-na watch 'em rise,___

Right be-fore___ my ver-y eyes.___

Biscuits in the oven, gonna watch 'em rise,
Biscuits in the oven, gonna watch 'em rise,
Biscuits in the oven, gonna watch 'em rise
Right before my very eyes.

When they get ready, gonna jump and shout,
When they get ready, gonna jump and shout,
When they get ready, gonna jump and shout,
Roll my eyes and bug them out. (Hey, hey!)

Gonna clap my hands and stomp my feet,
Clap my hands and stomp my feet,
Clap my hands and stomp my feet
Right before the very next beat.

CHORUS

Gonna look both ways when I cross the street. Left . . . right.
Gonna look both ways when I cross the street. Right . . . left.
Gonna look both ways when I cross the street. Left . . . right.
Gonna take my time when the light turns green.

CHORUS

Baking Biscuits

Be sure to ask an adult to help!

1 cup	all purpose flour	250 mL	1/3 cup	shortening	75 mL
1 cup	whole wheat flour	250 mL	3/4 cup	milk	200 mL
4 tsp.	baking powder	20 mL	1/3 cup	raisins	75 mL
3/4 tsp.	salt	4 mL			

1. Turn on the oven to 425°F (220°C) so it will heat up.

2. Sift the flour, baking powder, and salt together into a big bowl.

3. Mix in the shortening until the mixture looks like coarse bread crumbs.

4. Pour in the milk, add the raisins, and stir with a fork.

5. Put the dough on a lightly floured board. Knead very gently. Roll out to 1/2 inch (1.5 cm) thickness.

6. With a cookie cutter, cut out the biscuits.

7. Bake on an ungreased cookie sheet until light brown on top (12–15 minutes). Take carefully from the oven using oven mitts. Makes about 12 biscuits.

And remember: When you take some biscuits to share with your friends, look both ways when you cross the street!

Oats and Beans and Barley Grow

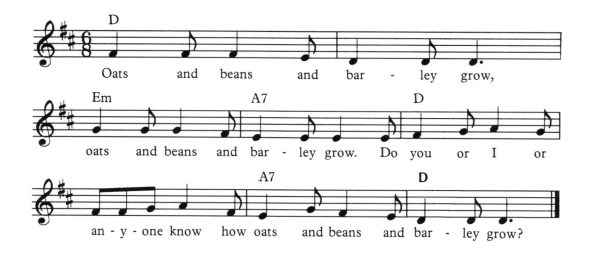

Oats and beans and bar - ley grow,
oats and beans and bar - ley grow. Do you or I or
an - y - one know how oats and beans and bar - ley grow?

Oats and beans and barley grow,
Oats and beans and barley grow,
Do you or I or anyone know
How oats and beans and barley grow?

First the farmer plants the seeds,
Stands up tall and takes his ease,
Stamps his feet and claps his hands
And turns around to view his land.

CHORUS

Then the farmer waters the ground,
Watches the sun shine all around,
Stamps his feet and claps his hands
And turns around to view his land.

CHORUS

To Watch the Magic . . . Grow Lima Beans

1. Stuff some paper towels into a jar or clear plastic cup.

2. Put two or three dried lima beans in between the side of the jar and the paper towels. Make sure they can't slip to the bottom.

3. Pour enough water into the jar to cover the bottom. (Add a little every day so the paper towels are always wet.)

4. Put the jar in a warm dark place, and take a peek each day to see what happens.

5. In a few days the beans will have roots. Now bring the jar into the light.

6. When there are stems and two sets of leaves the beans are ready to be replanted in soil.

Day-o

This song, sometimes called the "Banana Boat Song," originally came from the warm island of Trinidad. There, men and women worked hard during the cool night to load big bunches of bananas onto boats. The tallyman counted the bunches and paid the workers in the morning. Then they could go home to rest.

Day-o, me say day-o,
Daylight come and me wan' go home.
Day-o, me say day-o,
Daylight come and me wan' go home.

Work all night 'til the mornin' come, Daylight . . .
Stack banana 'til the mornin' come, Daylight . . .
Come, Mr. Tallyman, tally me banana, Daylight . . .
Me say come, Mr. Tallyman, tally me banana, Daylight . . .
Lift six hand, seven hand, eight hand bunch, Daylight . . .
Me say six hand, seven hand, eight hand bunch, Daylight . . .

Day-o, day-o, Daylight . . .
Day-o, day-o, Daylight . . .

A beautiful bunch o' ripe banana, Daylight . . .
A beautiful bunch o' ripe banana, Daylight . . .
Lift six hand, seven hand, eight hand bunch, Daylight . . .
Me say six hand, seven hand, eight hand bunch, Daylight . . .

Day, me say day-o, Daylight . . .
Day-o, day-o, Daylight . . .

Come, Mr. Tallyman, tally me banana, Daylight . . .
Me say come, Mr. Tallyman, tally me banana, Daylight . . .
Day-o, me say day-o, Daylight . . .
Day-o, me say day-o, Daylight . . .

Thanks a Lot

Thanks a lot,
Thanks for the sun in the sky.
Thanks a lot,
Thanks for the clouds so high.

Thanks a lot,
Thanks for the whispering wind.
Thanks a lot,
Thanks for the birds in the spring.

Thanks a lot,
Thanks for the moonlit night.
Thanks a lot,
Thanks for the stars so bright.

Thanks a lot,
Thanks for the wonder in me.
Thanks a lot,
Thanks for the way I feel.

Thanks for the animals, thanks for the land,
Thanks for the people everywhere.
Thanks a lot,
Thanks for all I've got,
Thanks for all I've got.

What have you got to say thanks for? Make up your own verse.

    Thanks a lot,
    Thanks for _____ _____ _____ _____ _____
    Thanks a lot,
    Thanks for _____ _____ _____ _____

To Everyone In All the World

To ev-ery-one in all the world_ I
A tous et cha-cun dans le monde_ je

reach my hand, I shake their hand._ To ev-ery-one in
tends la main, j'leur donne la main._ A tous et cha-cun

all the world_ I shake my hand like this.
dans le monde_ je donne la main comme ça.

Chorus

All, all to-geth-er, the whole wide world a-
Tous, tous en-sem-ble, au monde en-tier je

round, I may not know their lin-go, but
chante. C'est très fa-çile entre hu-mains, a-

I can say "By jin-go! No mat-ter where you
vec une poi-gnée de main, n'im-porte où dans le

live, we can shake hands."
monde, on peut s'en-tendre.

To everyone in all the world
I reach my hand, I shake their hand.
To everyone in all the world
I shake my hand like this.

All, all together,
The whole wide world around,
I may not know their lingo,
But I can say "By jingo,
No matter where you live
We can shake hands."

CHORUS

A tous et chacun dans le monde
Je tends la main, j'leur donne la main.
A tous et chacun dans le monde
Je donne la main comme ça.

Tous, tous ensemble, au monde entier je chante.
C'est très façile entre humains,
Avec une poignée de main,
N'importe où dans le monde, on peut s'entendre.

CHORUS

To everyone in all the world
I reach my hand, I shake their hand.
To everyone in all the world
I shake my hand like this.

All I Really Need

A friend asked me to write a song for the International Year of the Child in 1979. I thought about the things we all need to grow up healthy and happy. This song is for every child in the whole world.

All I really need is a song in my heart,
      food in my belly,
      and love in my family.
All I really need is a song in my heart
      and love in my family.

And I need the rain to fall,
And I need the sun to shine
To give life to the seeds we sow,
To give the food we need to grow.
All I really need is a song in my heart
      and love in my family.

CHORUS

And I need some clean water for drinking
And I need some clean air for breathing
So that I can grow up strong and
Take my place where I belong.
All I really need is a song in my heart
      and love in my family.

CHORUS

...love in my family,
...love in my family.

The Rights of the Child

Each child has the right:

to affection, love and understanding;

to adequate nutrition;

to learn to be a useful member of society and to develop individual abilities;

to be brought up in a spirit of peace and universal brotherhood.

The United Nations, 1979

Over in the Meadow

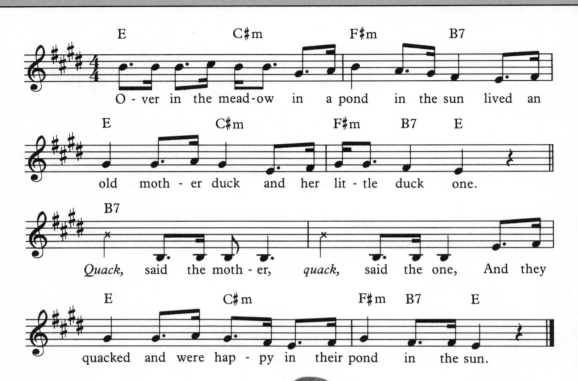

O - ver in the mead-ow in a pond in the sun lived an
old moth - er duck and her lit - tle duck one.
Quack, said the moth - er, *quack,* said the one, And they
quacked and were hap - py in their pond in the sun.

Over in the meadow in a pond in the sun
Lived an old mother duck and her little duck one.
Quack, said the mother, *quack,* said the one,
And they quacked and were happy in their pond in the sun.

Over in the meadow in a stream so blue
Lived an old mother fish and her little fish two.
Blub, said the mother, *blub, blub,* said the two,
And they swam and were happy in the stream so blue.

Over in the meadow in a nest in the tree
Lived an old mother bird and her birdies three.
Tweet, said the mother, *tweet, tweet, tweet,* said the three,
And they sang and were happy in their nest in the tree.

Over in the meadow on a rock by the shore
Lived an old mother frog and her little frogs four.
Ribit, said the mother, *ribit, ribit, ribit, ribit,* said the four,
And they croaked and were happy on the rock by the shore.

Over in the meadow in a big bee hive
Lived an old mother bee and her little bees five.
Bzz, said the mother, *bzz, bzz, bzz, bzz, bzz,* said the five,
And they buzzed and were happy in the big bee hive.

Over in the meadow in the noonday sun
There was a pretty mother and her baby one.
"Listen," said the mother, "to the ducks and the bees,
To the frogs and the fish and the birds in the trees."

Bzz, bzz, bzz, bzz, bzz, said the five,
Ribit, ribit, ribit, ribit, said the four,
Tweet, tweet, tweet, said the three,

Blub, blub, said the two,
Quack, said the one,
And the little baby laughed just to hear such fun!

All the animals from the song are in this picture. Find two ducks, three fish, four birds, five frogs, six bees and one human mother with her happy baby.

This Old Man

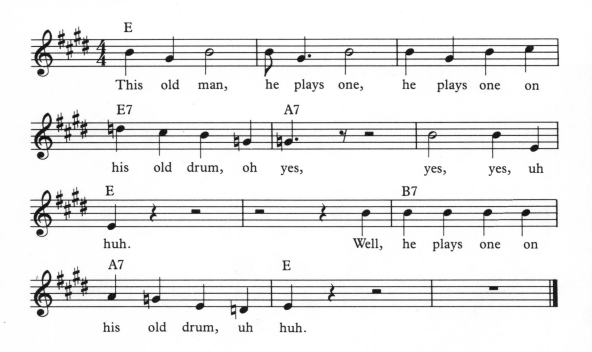

This old man, he plays one, he plays one on

his old drum, oh yes, yes, yes, uh

huh. Well, he plays one on

his old drum, uh huh.

33

You too can be a musician and join in with the old man's band. The children in the picture have found all sorts of things around the house to use in their band. See what you can find, or make your own instrument. For example, take an empty can or plastic bottle; drop in some uncooked rice, dried peas, or small stones; put on the lid and shake out the rhythm.

This old man, he plays one,
He plays one on his old drum, oh yes, yes, yes, uh huh.
Well, he plays one on his old drum, uh huh.

This old man, he plays two,
He plays two on his kazoo, oh yes, yes, yes, uh huh.
Oh, he plays two on his kazoo, uh huh.

This old man, he plays three,
He plays three on his ukulele, uh huh, yes, yes, uh huh.
He plays three on his ukulele, uh huh.

This old man, he plays four,
He plays four on his guitar, oh yes, yes, yes, uh huh.
Well, he plays four on his guitar, uh huh.

This old man, he plays five,
He plays five with his friend Clive, oh yes, yes, yes, uh huh.
Oh, he plays five with his friend Clive, uh huh.

This old man, he plays one,
This old man, he plays two,
This old man, he plays three,
This old man, he plays four,
This old man, he plays five,
Knick-knack! Paddywhack!

Water Dance

Kumbaya

Kum - ba - ya, Lord, kum - ba - ya,_____

Kum - ba - ya, Lord, kum - ba - ya,_____

Kum - ba - ya, Lord, kum - ba - ya,_____

Oh, Lord,___ kum - ba - ya._____

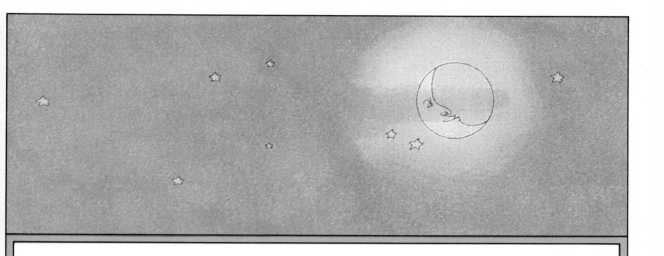

Kumbaya, Lord, kumbaya,
Kumbaya, Lord, kumbaya,
Kumbaya, Lord, kumbaya,
Oh, Lord, kumbaya.

Someone's praying, Lord, kumbaya,
Someone's praying, Lord, kumbaya,
Someone's praying, Lord, kumbaya,
Oh, Lord, kumbaya.

Someone's crying, Lord, kumbaya,
Someone's crying, Lord, kumbaya,
Someone's crying, Lord, kumbaya,
Oh, Lord, kumbaya.

Someone's singing, Lord, kumbaya,
Someone's singing, Lord, kumbaya,
Someone's singing, Lord, kumbaya,
Oh, Lord, kumbaya.

CHORUS

Oh, Lord, kumbaya.

If you say the words "come by here" to yourself over and over, you will know what "kumbaya" means. This song was sung long ago in East Africa. Now people all over the world enjoy singing it, especially on a starry night around a campfire.

Joshua Giraffe

Joshua Giraffe was born in a zoo; he lived there too.
For two years and a half he hasn't had a bath.

   "My mommy doesn't lick me, even when I'm sticky from
      candy floss, candy apples, popcorn,
        soft drinks, jelly beans and gumdrops.
There must be something better than living in this cage.
But I'm really not too sure, 'cause I'm rather short of age."

Joshua Giraffe was feeling kind of sad; things were going bad. How little of life he'd had, wasting away with no room to play; trapped in a zoo with buffalo poo. So he went next door to the elephant, and he asked him what to do.

"I'm wasting away with no room to play. I'm trapped in a zoo with buffalo poo."

The elephant was very old and grey, and he had a huge balloon bottom. And he said:

"Never fear, Joshua, for a vision will appear!"

That night a dream came to Joshua. And Joshua saw animals like:

      crazy monkeys...
      and a whole pile of hippie potosteropouses...
      and flitty moths...
      and frogs, size 12...
      and sleazy lizards...
      and a tribe of nasty saviars!

But Joshua wasn't afraid, 'cause he sang himself this song:

      Nothing can go wrongo, I'm in the Congo....
      Nothing can go wrongo, I'm in the Congo....

But even in his dream he knew he'd never get away, not even for a day. Then . . .

A peanut hit him on the nose.

Joshua Giraffe was back in the zoo. What could he do? Awakened from his dream, he'd never be the same because of things he'd seen. He'd seen:
> alligators, crocodiles, tree sloths,
> anacondas, cobras, and large-winged moths;
> orangutangs, gorillas, baboons eating grapes,
> gibbons, rude mandrills, and just plain apes!

But Joshua was lucky, he had some special friends. And that day they went to the zoo. He was uptight, so they waited 'til the night and they chopped his cage in two. He discovered he could fly, and he soared into the sky with them wrapped around his neck. And they haven't come back yet. So if you see them, get a net . . . foo-ni-chel-lo, ho-ho ho-ho-ho-ho-ho ho-ho-ho ho-ho-ho. . . .

That's right, they haven't come back yet. But when they do, they say they're going to free all the animals from their cages, no matter how new or modern – and even some pets too! So if on your way home today you happen to find:
> a baboon basking in the balcony,
> or a lion licking a lemon in the lobby,
> or a python perched in the pantry,
> a wildebeast in the w.c.
> with a turtle twirling in your tub –

don't be afraid. Just say that you're a friend of their friend, Joshua Giraffe. Joshua, Joshua, Joshua Giraffe, Joshua, Joshua. . . .

Morningtown Ride

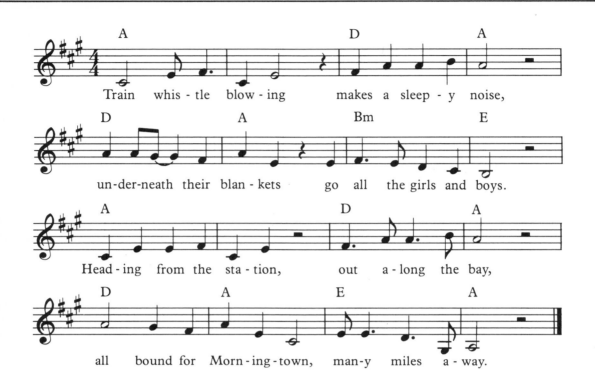

Train whis-tle blow-ing makes a sleep-y noise,
un-der-neath their blan-kets go all the girls and boys.
Head-ing from the sta-tion, out a-long the bay,
all bound for Morn-ing-town, man-y miles a-way.

Train whistle blowing makes a sleepy noise,
Underneath their blankets go all the girls and boys.
Heading from the station, out along the bay,
All bound for Morningtown, many miles away.

Sarah's at the engine, Tony rings the bell,
John swings the lantern, to show that all is well.
Rocking, rolling, riding, out along the bay,
All bound for Morningtown, many miles away.

Maybe it is raining where our train will ride,
But all the little travellers are snug and warm inside.
Somewhere there is sunshine, somewhere there is day,
Somewhere there is Morningtown, many miles away.